## Introduction

Back in March of 2020, we all suddenly found ourselves with a lot of extra time on our hands. How we chose to spend that time varied wildly. I decided to spend mine in three areas, photography, writing, and productivity. Spanning two of those areas, I did a deep dive from a beginner's perspective in one of my favorite productivity tools, Notion. Over the course of a few weeks, I wrote and published four articles to take new users from a blank slate to some usable pages.

Those articles became my most successful articles on Medium of all time. I have had a lot of requests for more articles and clarification on some of the earlier work. So, I decided to combine everything into this mini-course. Thousands of people read the first four articles for free on Medium, but since most of those readers came from outside Medium, I made about $3 for all my work.

That is one of the reasons for this mini-course. I could lie and say it if for the good of the people or some altruistic crap, but I put a lot of time and effort into these articles and wouldn't mind making a buck.

So, thank you for purchasing and I hope you learn something. You can contact me at the same email you used to purchase this course with any and all questions, and I promise to answer each one.

Thank you,

Darryl

# DAY ONE

Notion is probably the most amazing productivity tool to come on the market since the spreadsheet. Certainly, it's the most amazing since Evernote, and that's been ten years. But on first opening it up, most people, including myself, look at the screen and wonder what to do next.

Just getting to that first screen is a challenge.

The metaphor you will hear most often about Notion is comparing it to a box of Legos. This is a good analogy as far as it goes.

Notion is a bunch of blocks you can build stuff with. But I take the example a bit further.

Notion is like a box of Legos if you have never seen, or heard of, Legos in your life.

No, that's not quite it, either. Notion is like someone dumped a box of Legos, Tinker Toys, Lincoln Logs, and an erector set on the floor in front of you and said, "Build something."

Eventually, you will figure some things out, but that will be after a lot of staring at the pile and many false starts.

And that is the reason for the myriad of how-to tutorials and videos on the web today. But almost all of them are the same. They start with a hugely complicated screen, while the podcaster says, "Here is my entire life in Notion," and then proceeds to click on pages, and links and databases, and calendars, and five minutes later, you are back staring at that blank screen again. If you even got that far.

No one tells you how to actually get started with the app. Notion's own Start Here page assumes you have already started. This tutorial will get you to that first page. In the next, we will work on that blank page.

You aren't going to learn much in this first tutorial, and you aren't going to get very far. But you will get started. I will walk through the on-boarding process and get to that blank screen, and give you something to play with. And sometimes, that's all it takes. Don't worry about making mistakes. If you are like most people, you will find yourself starting over.

Several times.

The first thing you need to do, so you will be able to stare at that blank page, is get Notion. To do this, browse over to **Notion**. You can download the app for desktop and mobile, but for now, just enter your email address. Notion works the same in the web version as the desktop version, so it is easier just to start with the web version until you are sure you want to go further.

Now is probably a good time to discuss the cost. To start, Notion is free, and I strongly suggest you use the free version as long as you can. Originally that got you up to 1,000 blocks. At this point, you don't have an understanding of what blocks are or how quickly you will need them, which is why it's a good thing Notion changed that a few months ago. Now, the free plan has unlimited blocks. You may not know what that means yet, but trust me, it's good. It also means you will probably never need to pay for the plan.

If you do decide to upgrade later, the paid plan, is only $4 a month. This gets you unlimited guests, unlimited file size uploads and a version history of 30 days. If you are a solo user, only the file size might be a problem. At $4 a month, it's still one of the most inexpensive apps in its league.

Either way, you end up on the same screen. Enter your email address and click Get Started.

When you enter your email, you get the following screen. Go to your email and retrieve the login code they sent you and paste it into the box. As you can see, if you have a Google account, you van log in with that. This is what I did, but the end result is the same.

# Sign Up

G Continue with Google

EMAIL

myemail@domain.com

We just sent you a temporary login code.
Please check your inbox.

Paste login code

Continue with Login Code

On the following screen, you need to enter your name and role. The role will only control the suggested templates that they offer in a couple of pages. This is one of those discouraging points you will encounter in the on-boarding process. We aren't going to use templates at this time, so just choose Personal. You can add a photo, but you may as well wait until later, as you can do that at any time.

## Welcome! First things first...

Tell us a bit about yourself.

Add a photo

First Name

Ada

Last Name

Lovelace

Role

Select Role

- 🎨 Design
- 📕 Education
- 🔨 Engineering
- 👫 Human Resources
- 🔧 Marketing
- 😊 Personal
- 💼 Product Management
- ♡ Sales
- 🚙 Support

On the next page, give your workspace a name. A workspace is the highest level of the hierarchy in your notion account. I only have one, which I gave my first name. Most people will only have one workspace, and there is no reason to have more than one until you are a much more advanced user. Assuming you are using this for yourself, select Just Me for your Team Size and continue.

The next page discusses templates, without really telling you what they are, or how to use them. Templates are great once you have an idea of what you want to do, but are just confusing for the complete beginner. Note Personal in the drop-down box. This is the role you selected earlier. You can change that here to get a feel for the templates offered, but when you are done, change it back to Personal and click Start without templates.

Notion opens up a view you will become familiar with and gives you a first page, called Get Started. Again, Notion has given you some stuff you don't really know what to do with, but it's as good a place as any to play around, so we will do that. Then we will delete this and get to that famous and aforementioned, blank page.

First, let's look around the screen. The area on the left is called the Sidebar. This is where a lot of your navigation will take place. As you add pages, they will appear there. At the top is your workspace name. You can click on it to download the apps or log out.

Below that are three menu items that will always be there, a quick find, updates, and settings. Quick Find is just that, and the primary tool for finding things anywhere in your workspace. All Updates is kind of a history of everything you have done and when you did it. Below that is settings, where a few basic settings are located. You won't need any of this until much later.

Next is the listing for the two pages that they created, and below that, three more menu items we will explore in another lesson. At the bottom of the sidebar is the New Page button, which, you guessed it, is one way of creating a new page. We won't be using that, either.

The large area on the right is called a page. This is the main building block of Notion and where you will spend most of your time. In the upper right, are more menu items that you won't need until later.

The center of this page is where we will focus for now. Each of the items on the page, in Notion's language, is called a block. If you have ever worked with Wordpress, you are probably familiar with the concept. There are text blocks, checkboxes, an embedded gif, and a subpage. Follow the instructions on each line to get a feel for the basic mechanics.

For now, there are three main takeaways:
Everything is a block, and each block can be dragged around.
Pages can be dragged into any order and nested within other pages.

If you right-click on the dot-menu to the left of any item, you can see that you can turn anything into anything else. (For the most part).

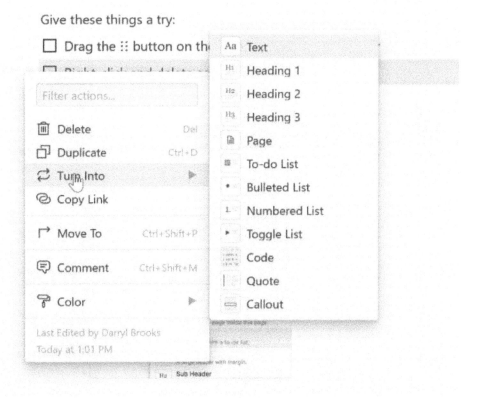

Play around with the page until you are completely confused. When you are happy with that, click on the three-dot menu to the right of Get Started on the Sidebar, and click Delete. You are going to have to tell it two more times that you really, really, really want to delete this page.

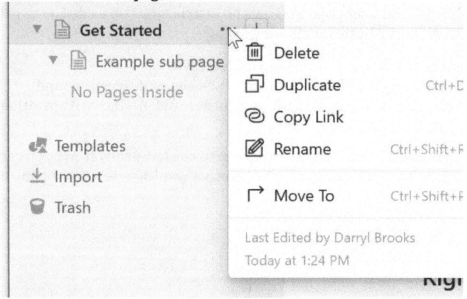

Finally! We are on that blank page.
And this is where we will leave it until the next lesson.

# DAY TWO

Welcome back to the second installment of my How to Use Notion course. In the first of the series, you learned how to get the software, sign up, and took a brief tour around the screen.
On day two, we will take a deeper dive around the initial screen and look at all the menus and links.

So, log in, and let's return to that proverbial blank page and get started. Note that this is only a test account I am using to write this series. At some point, I'll pull back the curtain on my real account and let you see more about how I am using Notion.

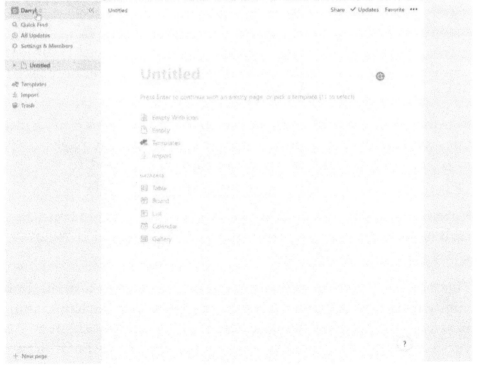

At the top left is your workspace name. You can change that later if you want, but this course will assume you are a solo user, so it doesn't matter what you name your workspace. Clicking on it is only useful for downloading the apps or for logging out. That link is a good place to grab the desktop app, but you will probably want to get the mobile apps directly from your mobile app store.

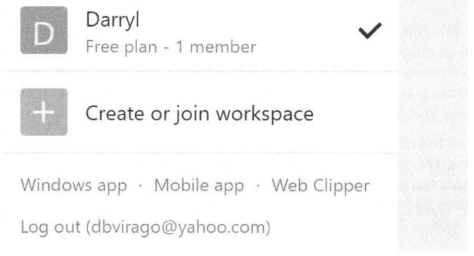

In this example, the software knows I am on Windows. I assume if you are on Mac, that option would be displayed. If not, here is the link to getting Notion for the Mac.

Beneath that, Quick Find brings up an excellent search function for your Notion pages. However, because I built my pages carefully (and rebuilt as I learned more), I rarely need to use the search. But it's there if you need it and does a great job.

**Note for those of you coming from Evernote: At this time, Notion does not search the contents of PDF files, but it is something they are working on.**

This brings up a great point. The team at Notion is a small, but highly dedicated group that is working hard to make Notion the best productivity software out there. I have found them to be very helpful, responsive, and transparent, unlike most of its competitors.

The next menu item is Settings & Members. The observant among you will note I did not attempt to hide my email address. You should know, however, this is an address I use only as a spam trap or for testing things like this Notion account. I never check the mail there. If you do need to reach out to me, you can email me here.

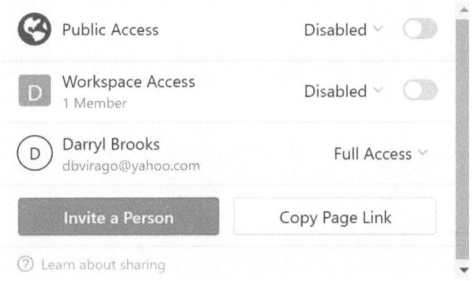

When you click on Settings and Members, the above window opens with the Members page highlighted. Again, since this tutorial will assume a single user, you will not need to use this page, so let's start with My Account.

## Personal info

EMAIL
dbvirago@yahoo.com   Change email

FIRST NAME
Darryl

LAST NAME
Brooks

## Password

You can set a permanent password if you don't want to use temporary login codes.

Change password

Remove password

## Calendar

Start week on Monday
This will change how all calendars in your app look.

## Danger zone

Delete my account

Update   Cancel

As you can see, this just lets you change a few personal account items, and you will likely never need to come back here unless… Creating, playing with, and fine-tuning your Notion account is an iterative process. You will likely make many false starts, and while it is easy to delete pages and move things around, if you get really frustrated, you can always delete your account and start over. However, it would make much more sense to create a new workspace, move over what you like and start fresh that way. But we are getting ahead of ourselves.

My Notifications only has relevance for people on teams, so we won't go into that.

My Connected Apps allows you to connect other apps for bringing over, or linking to, your other data easily. We will return to importing and embedding in another lesson, but as you will see in the next screen, if you are an Evernote user, connecting that app has additional benefits.

Next is the Earn Credit screen. Using Notion is free. Depending on what you want to do, it may be enough forever, but it will certainly give you enough room to decide if it is worth the $4 a month fee.

You are given $5 just for signing up and using the web version, and you can earn credit by all the ways listed below

Before you do that, look at all the ways you can earn credit at the bottom. Without much effort, you should be able to rack up $25-$30 in credit, depending on whether you use Evernote. If you are an Evernote user, note that you only have to import something, not everything. Importing from Evernote will be a separate topic, but know that even if you think you want to import everything from Evernote, you should do it slowly and one folder at a time. So, in short, to get that credit, connect your Evernote account, import a folder with one doc in it, and ka-ching.

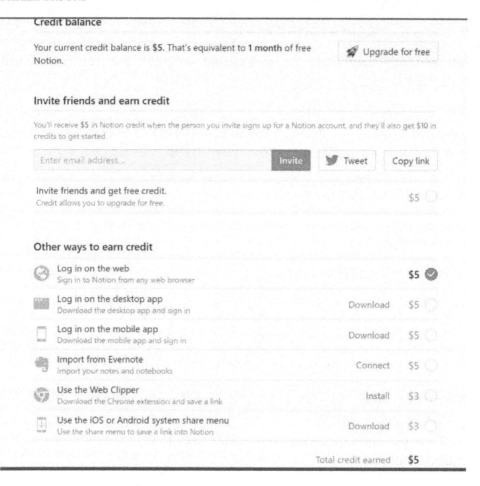

**Update: Note that the Invite Friends link is no longer there, since the plan is now free for everyone.**

The Settings menu option has several useful features.

**Name**

Darryl

You can use your name or the name of your team. Keep it simple.

**Icon**

D

Upload an image or pick an emoji. It will show up in your sidebar and notifications.

**Domain**

www.notion.so/ URL

Share the link to add anyone with an allowed email domain to your workspace.

**Allowed Email Domains**

Type an email domain...

Anyone with email addresses at these domains can automatically join your workspace.

**Export Content**

Export All Workspace Content

The Name, at the top, is the name you gave to the workspace on **Day One**, and you can change it at any time.

Below that is a space for an icon, you can upload. This would be displayed at the top of the navigation bar next to the workspace name. As you will learn as we move forward, Notion is a very visual app, full of emojis, icons, and images. At some point, you will probably want to include an icon. On my real page, I just added a picture of myself.

The next two options are again, for team use only. The final option on the page, is a link to Export Content. **Here** is a link to a lot of information about exporting your workspace, but basically, you have an option of PDF, HTML, or Markdown/CSV formats. PDF is only available for Enterprise versions of the software. Once you click on it, Notion will email you a link when the download is ready.

How long this takes will depend on how much content you have. I suggest a two-pronged approach to backing up Notion. First, always keep copies of important documents in at least two other places. This can be Evernote, Google Docs, OneDrive, or whatever backup system you employ for your digital assets. Second, periodically do both an HTML and a Markup version of your Notion database, so you can recreate it if disaster strikes.
I have no personal knowledge of Notion ever losing any data, but I still think it's your responsibility to maintain adequate protection.
Upgrade gives you a brief overview of the costs and options on the different plans. You will be using the free plan for the near future, and hopefully, upgrade to the personal plan once you get rolling.

The security features are only for Enterprise users. Dark Mode simply toggles dark mode on for those that prefer it. Below that will be a running tally of how many of your free blocks you have used. That tally will disappear if you have a paid plan. Then there are two options concerning upgrading to a paid plan. That's it for the Settings and Members. Here is another shot of the navigation bar, so you don't have to scroll back up to the full screenshot.

HOW TO GET STARTED WITH NOTION

D Darryl ⌄

Q  Quick Find

🕒  All Updates

⚙  Settings & Members

▶  🗋  **Untitled**

📇  Templates

⬇  Import

🗑  Trash

Between Settings and Templates will be all of your pages. Currently, you only have one blank page, appropriately titled Untitled, but that will change soon. I promise.

Maybe not today, but soon.

Templates is a magical place that we will return to after you've gotten a feel for what Notion can do. Trust me. Going there now will either confuse you or send you down a rabbit hole from which there is no return.

Import will bring up a dialog of all the places from which you can directly import data into Notion.

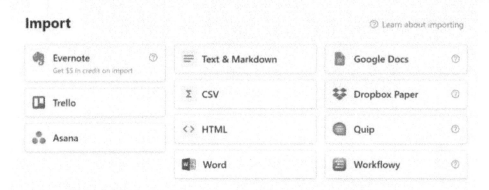

We will cover some of these in future editions, but know that you can bring over your information from a variety of sources.

Trash shouldn't need a description. **Here** is a much more in-depth explanation, but just know that, with a few exceptions, you can get back things you delete. Those exceptions, as you may have seen on **Day One**, require triple confirmation.

Down at the lower-left corner of the screen is a New page button. You can probably guess what that does, but there are several other and better ways to create a new page, which we will cover later.

The Share button on the upper right has several options:

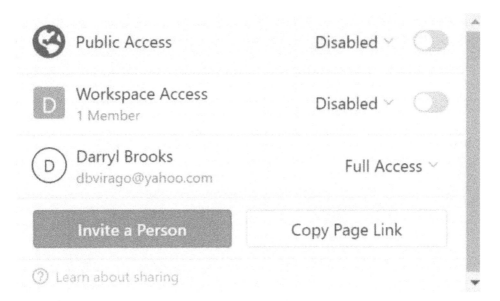

Most of this is, once again, for teams. The only exceptions are Copy Page Link and Public Access.

Copy Page Link is mostly for internal use, and there is a much easier way to do that. If you hover over Public Access, you are given a bit more information and can see that you could give someone a link to a page and make it public. I've personally never done that, but you have the option to do so.

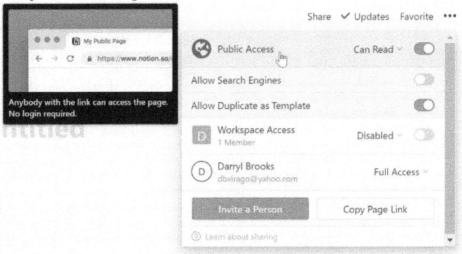

Updates, as discussed on **Day One**, will show you the entire history of what you have done. Kind of scary, but there it is.
Favorite will move a copy of the link to the top of your navigation bar. You will want to do this with a few select pages you use often. Here is a screenshot, and you probably know when we will come back to that.
Later.

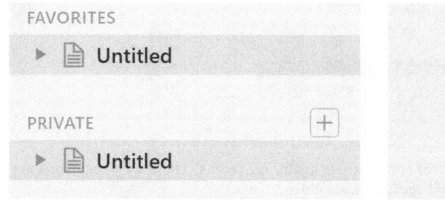

The three-dot menu is there on every page and gives you information and formatting options for that particular page. One thing of note for now, at the bottom, is where you can get the word count for any page you are working on. This is useful for writers. The one shown is the word count for this article at the start of this paragraph.

STYLE                                    STYLE

Ag    Ag    Ag              Ag    Ag    Ag
Default  Serif   Mono         Default  Serif   Mono

Small Text            ◯⬤      Small Text            ◯
Full Width            ◯⬤      Full Width            ◯

Page Lock             ◯⬤      Page Lock             ◯

☆  Add to Favorites           ☆  Add to Favorites
🔗  Copy Link                  🔗  Copy Link

↶  Undo          Ctrl+Z       ↶  Undo          Ctrl+Z
🕘  Page History   UPGRADE      🕘  Page History   UPGRADE
🗑  Delete                     🗑  Delete

↓  Import                     ↓  Import
📎  Export                     📎  Export
    PDF, HTML, Markdown            PDF, HTML, Markdown

↱  Move To     Ctrl+Shift+P    ↱  Move To     Ctrl+Shift+P

Word Count: 1848               Word Count: 1848

Last Edited by Darryl Brooks    Last Edited by Darryl Brooks
Today at 11:15 AM               Today at 11:15 AM

At the bottom right, behind the ? is a help menu. There are several help related subjects there, but I want you to remember the Keyboard shortcuts as we will return to that....

Help & support guide 📖

Send us a message 💬

Keyboard shortcuts

What's new?

Join us

Twitter – @NotionHQ

Terms & privacy

Status

Notion 2.7.22.1.10
Updated 15 hours ago

And that's a wrap on day two.

Whew! We covered a lot of stuff today, and we still have a blank page.
But I promise, on the next installment, we will start putting stuff on it.

Promise.

# DAY THREE

Welcome back to the third installment of my How to Use Notion course. In the first of the series, you learned how to get the software, sign up, and a brief tour around the screen.

In the second chapter, we took a deeper dive around your initial screen and looked at all the menus and links.

Today, we will finally start putting some stuff on that blank page you've been staring at.

So, log in, and let's get started.

But, first…

There's always a gotcha, isn't there?

The conventional wisdom is that before you start working with Notion, you decide what you want to do with it. And that's part of the problem with Notion, because it can be a:
Wiki
Dashboard
Journal
Project Manager
Notetaker
Content Creation (One of the things I am using it for)
Or any combination of these things and a whole lot more. And it can present this information in databases, different views of those databases, on pages, with graphics, or again, any combination.
So, with all that said, how do you begin? Again, conventional wis-

dom says you sit down with a blanks sheet of paper and start plotting out what you want to do. Once you have a rough idea, you can begin converting that into Notion pages.

But that's not what we're going to do.

I think until you get an idea of the power and flexibility of Notion, you are going to have a hard time conceptualizing how to use it. So we are going to start throwing stuff up on that blank page, changing it, moving it around, and adding to it.

And when we're done, you are most likely going to throw it all out and start over.

But you will do some with some knowledge and a little bit of experience.

So, let's go back to that blank page.

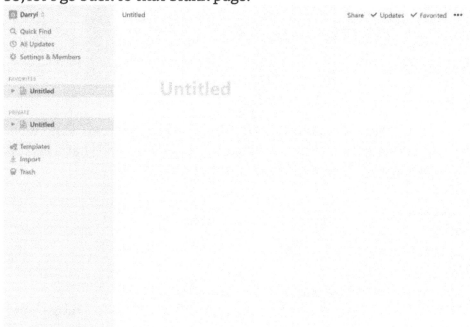

First, let's give the page a title and dress it up a bit. Call it whatever you want to, but don't spend too much time thinking about it.

I'm going to call it First Page because I'm clever like that.
Now, hover your cursor near the title you just typed, and you will
see three links appear above it.

☺ Add icon   🖼 Add cover   💬 Add discussion

# First Page

Add discussion is more for team use, so we will ignore that. The
other two are for resources that you should take advantage of
often, Add icon and Add cover.
Each page in Notion can have an icon or emoji, as well as a cover
image. Notion is very much a graphical interface, so you should
take advantage of these. But it's not just to look good. The icons
can make navigation easier once you have a lot of pages. Here are
the icons associated with some of my current pages.

- ▶ 🏠 Home
- ▶ 📪 Inbox
- ▶ 📝 Writing
- ▶ 📷 Photography
- ▶ 🏠 House
- ▶ 🏅 Health and Fitness
- ▶ 💲 Financial
- ▶ 🚀 Travel
- ▼ 📺 Entertainment

As your sidebar fills up, not using icons will leave it as just a column of words. The icons make pages easy to identify and find. On your blank page, click on Add icon. A random icon will appear. In the unlikely event that you like it, that's fine. If not, click on it, and a scrollable window will open with a ton of emojis.

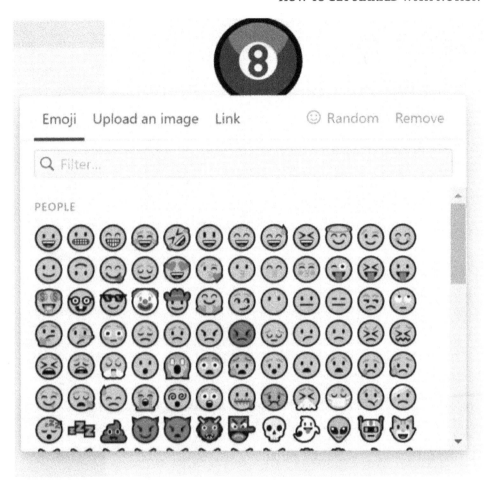

You can also upload your own or link to one on the web. There are a lot of resources you can link to for icons, but now, scroll through the list and pick one. Since this is our first page, I'm going to pick a hand showing number one.

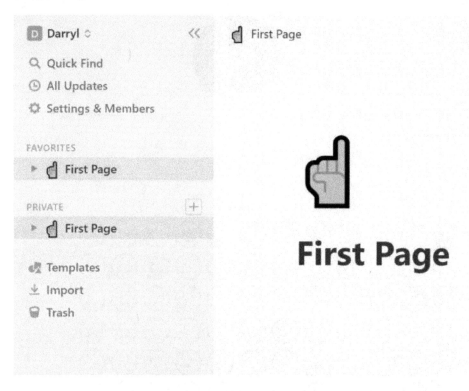

Notice, once you choose an icon, it shows above the title, on the header of the page, and beside the names in the sidebar.

(Remember we added the page as a favorite, so that's why it shows up twice.)

Next, we will add a cover image. Again, you don't have to do this, but it can add fun, color, inspiration, or most anything else to each page. I encourage you to make your Notion fit your personality. If you're like me, you will spend a lot of time here, so it may as well represent you.

Move your cursor back up and click on Add cover. Again, Notion will choose a random image from its library, but we are going to change that again.

If you hover over the cover, you will see Change cover and Reposition. We will get back to reposition in a minute. Click on Change cover.

This will bring up several options; Gallery, Upload, Link, and Unsplash.

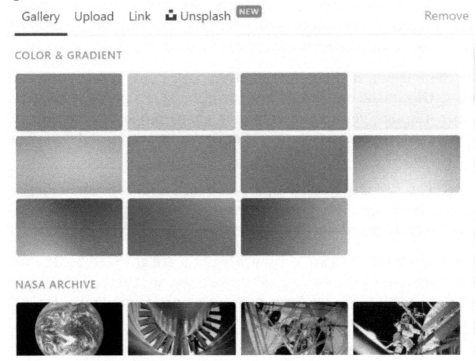

Click on Gallery to take a look at the images that are built into Notion. In addition to the blank color graphics, Notion includes some very cool photos from NASA, a few patterns from the Met Museum, some images from the Rijks Museum, Japanese prints from the Met, and some random art from the Met. You can click on any of these to replace the random cover.

You can also click on Upload to add your image. Since I am a photographer, I have done some of that. You can also link to an image somewhere on the web, but first, make sure you have the right to use it, and second, know that if that link breaks, your image will disappear.

The most exciting choice is the new Unsplash link. Unsplash is a website where many artists and photographers, including myself, have donated images for use in any way you choose. Click on the link, and it will bring up a scrollable selection from which to choose.

But the real power of Unsplash is the search function. I entered First Page and came up with a small selection.

Pro Tip: If you find the small thumbnails hard to read, you can go to Unsplash.com and do your search there. Once you find the perfect image, you can download it, then upload it to Notion, or better yet, return to Notion, enter the same search and find your selection.

With the search window open, you can click on, and try out different images. When you are happy, click away from the window to close it and finalize your choice.

Pro Tip: Clicking away is something you are going to be doing a lot. Any time I window, page, pop-up, or anything else is open in Notion, click somewhere else in Notion, or click-away as it's called, to close that window.

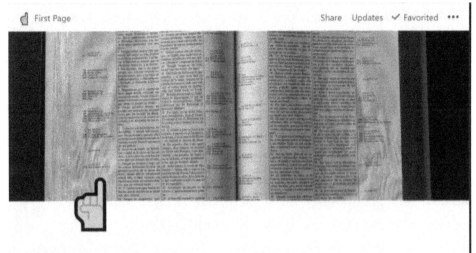

## First Page

As you can see, I picked an open book to illustrate our first page, but I'd like it to show the top of the book. Hover over the image, click on Reposition, and then drag the image until you are happy. Click Save postion, and you're done.

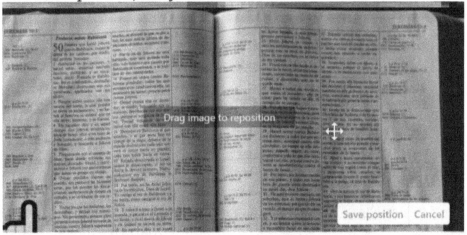

I urge you to get creative and use both the icon and cover image on all of your pages. This will customize your Notion setup and make it your own.

### Blocks

What are blocks? If you have ever used Wordpress or a similar site or software, you are probably familiar with the concept. If you are not, blocks are the building blocks of Notion. You just created your first page. A page is a block. Anything except the title, icon, or cover image you put on a page is a block.

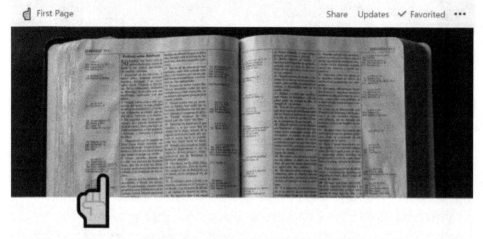

Notion allows **unlimited** blocks on its free plan.

So, let's take a look at creating a block. The prompt for creating a new block will always look the same. There will always be one at the bottom of the page, and between any blocks where you have left a space. The prompt has three parts, the + sign, the six-dot menu, and the prompt to start typing with a '/.'

Hover over the plus, and you get a pop-up that says, Click to add a block below. Do that, and a scrollable window comes up with all of the options for blocks. We will discuss the different types of blocks as we come to them, but for now, just scroll down and take a look. As you scroll, notice that the window keeps filling up with more types of blocks. Notion is adding new blocks all the time.

That is just one way of adding blocks, and is the way you will probably add them until you get more familiar. We will return to the six-dot menu after we create our first block. But first, let's look at the second way to add a new block (there are three). At the prompt, type a / and notice how the same window of blocks shows up. After you have used Notion a while, you will use this a lot. The reason is that, once you type the / and begin typing letters, the choice will narrow down, so this will be a faster way of adding a block.

Let's add a Heading 1 to see how this works. First, click the + sign, then click Heading 1. Note now that the block label has changed to say Heading 1. Start typing there to produce a block then hit enter.

# First Page

## This is a Heading 1

+ :: Type '/' for commands

Congratulations, you have created a block. Now, with your cursor on the next line, type /h2, and hit enter. You notice as you started typing the h, the highlight in the block window dropped from Text to Heading, then at the 2, only the H2 heading was showing.

When you hit enter, you are producing an H2 block.

# First Page

## This is a Heading 1

### This is a Heading 2

+ :: Type '/' for commands

So, here is how it usually goes when producing blocks until you get much more familiar with the software. If you aren't sure what kind of block you want or what it is called, click the + and pick it from the list. If you know the name, use the / command, followed by the first letters to jump to it quickly.

Once you get more familiar, you will begin using more keyboard shortcuts. To take a look at them, click the ? in the bottom-right corner, and select Keyboard Shortcuts from the menu. People that are heavy Notion users do almost everything with keyboard shortcuts, but it is better to learn one of them at a time as you need them.

For instance, I use the Toggle List block type a lot. I could start typing /tog, and it will pop up, but I know if I type the > followed by a space on a new line, the toggle just appears.
Before the next chapter, I want you to play with adding different types of blocks, but before I go, we need to talk about that six-dot menu, mostly so you'll know how to clean up this mess we're making.

First, know that all blocks can be moved around. That is one of the great things about blocks. Whether it's a word, a sentence, a paragraph, or a page, click and drag on the six-dot menu to drag and drop it someplace else.

Click and drag Heading 2 above Heading 1. You will notice the blue horizontal line pop up, showing you where you are dropping it. If you don't see a line, you can't drop it there.

# First Page

## This is a Heading 2

# This is a Heading 1

For instance, try and drag it above the title, and you can't. While you were dragging, you may have noticed a small vertical blue line. This is because some blocks can be dragged next to others, creating columns. Drag your two blocks around to get a feel for this. You will be doing it a lot.

## This is a Heading 2

## This is a Heading 1

Now, click on the six-dot menu to get this pop-up.

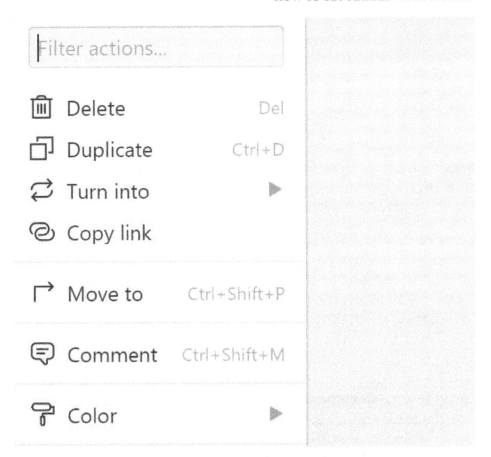

Here, you can do a lot of things with the particular block you clicked on. For now, the one we want to use is Delete. When you have played with creating and dragging blocks, use the Delete command to get rid of them and get back to the blank page.

That's where we will start next week.

Until then, have fun, play with blocks, and let me know if you have any questions.

# DAY FOUR

Welcome back to the fourth installment of my How to Use Notion course. So far, we downloaded and installed the software, took a brief tour and learned about working with blocks.

To be honest, that's all you need to know to get started and you can go a long way with no further knowledge. But today we will do a dive into one of the most useful features of Notion, databases. If you have used **Airtable** , then you are familiar with how databases work in Notion. Both products have similar implementations, and the basic concepts are almost identical. If you have any experience with databases on any platform, then the concept will be familiar, but the execution is a bit different. If you are familiar with spreadsheets, you should be right at home, but Notion databases offer a lot more.

For the database purists out there, you will excuse me for using the terms database and tables interchangeably. I know they are not the same thing, but Notion uses it that way in their documentation, so I will follow suit.

I have been working on a database to track my articles on Medium, so that is what we will build in this tutorial.

So log in and let's get started.

You may have left some blocks in place from the last lesson, but we will create our tables on new pages, so click the New page icon. For this example, we will Title the page Medium Articles, then click the Table icon under Database.

# Medium Articles

Press Enter to continue with an empty page, or pick a template
(↑↓ to select)

📄 Empty with icon

🗋 Empty

🎨 Templates

⤓ Imports

DATABASE

⊞ Table

⊞ Board

⊞ List

📆 Calendar

⊞ Gallery

We want this to be a full-page table rather than inline. We will create inline views of it in the next chapter. When you click on Table, a blank table appears with the default values. Each column is a property of the table. In traditional database terms, these would be field names. A Notion table will always have a name property that is of type Title. You can't change or delete this field, but you can change the name of the field. Click on the field to get a drop-down window of options.

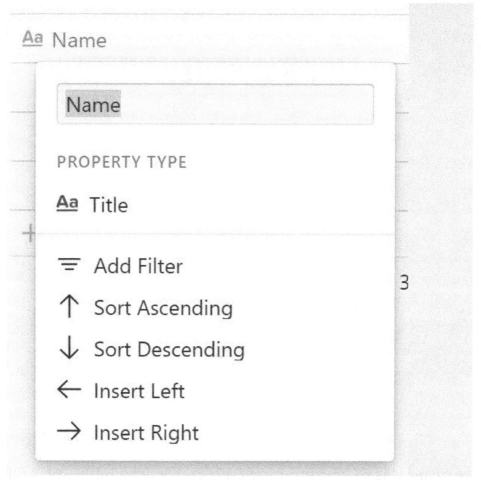

We will change the name of the field to Title and leave the rest alone. My table has many columns, but for this example, we need to just change the other two given to you. We will add more columns later when we get to relations.

The next field is Tags, which is a Multi-Select type and is useful for anyone accustomed to using tags for searches. For this tutorial, we will change the name to Creation Date and the type to Date. Click on the column name as before and change the name, then hover over the Property Type field to get another pop-up.

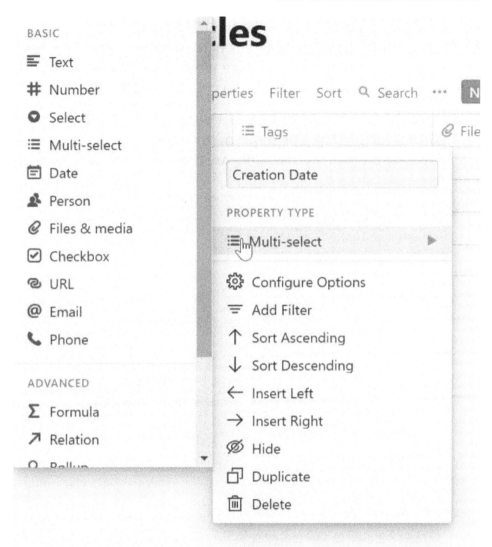

Click on the Date type in the pop-up window. In the same way, change the Files field name to Status and make the type, Select. Congratulations! You have created your first table in Notion. Build whatever type table you have a need for similarly and add some data to it. In our example, we will create a second table called Publications.

I will switch to my live data for the rest of this article. As shown in the screenshot, create a second table the same way you made the Articles table and add the fields and field types shown below. Note that now I am using the Tags field, which is a multi-select, while Type is a single select. These kinds of fields are handy for repetitive data, so you don't have to type it in more than once.

Add some data as shown, or play with your own tables. Next, we will add a relationship. For those of you that have a fear of relationships, I apologize, but not only are they great in life but are invaluable in databases.

# Publications

⊞ Name ˅

| Aa Name | # Followers | ◉ Type | ☰ Subjects | ☰ Tags |
|---|---|---|---|---|
| a Few Words | 2,992 | Draft | | Life Lessons  Motiviation  Productivity  Writing  Self-Improvement |
| Ascent | 89,000 | Draft | Personal, inspirational | Self-Improvement  Self  Personal Growth  Personal Development  Life Lessons |
| Bad Influence | 1,344 | Draft | | |
| Be Unique | 754 | Draft | | Love  Success  Fiction  Life  Health |
| Be Yourself | 158,000 | Draft | | |

Now, head back over to the articles database and create a new field called Publication. We will use this field to designate what, if any, publication has produced our articles. But instead of typing it in or using a Select field, we will build a relationship to tie it back into the Publications table. So, in the Property Type, scroll most of the way to the bottom and select Relation.

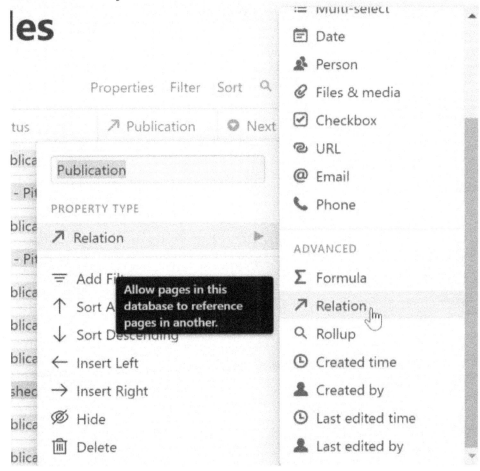

You will then get a pop-up telling you to Create a relation to another database. Click in the Select a Database box and another pop-up appears with all of your tables, in this case, just two. Choose Publications.

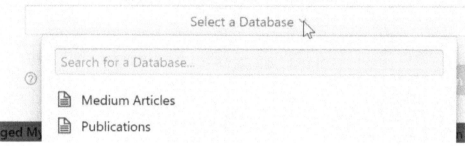

### Create a relation to another database

A relation allows you to link pages from other databases.

Select a Database

Search for a Database...

📄 Medium Articles

📄 Publications

Now, in the articles table, if you click on the Publications field, a pop-up will appear showing you all the fields in the Publication Database. Select the Publication you want and it will appear for your article.

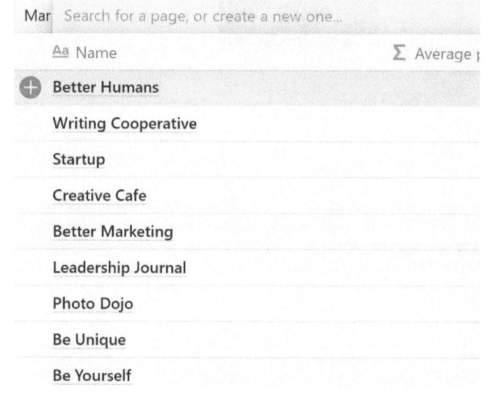

Search for a page, or create a new one...

Aa Name                                          Σ Average

➕ **Better Humans**

**Writing Cooperative**

**Startup**

**Creative Cafe**

**Better Marketing**

**Leadership Journal**

**Photo Dojo**

**Be Unique**

**Be Yourself**

You may wonder, why go to all that trouble; why not just enter the name of the Publication into the Articles table? There are two reasons for this. First, there is a concept in database management called normalization. What this means is that you never want to have repeating data in two tables. It's not only a waste of space (this goes back to the days when storage was at a premium), but it's difficult to maintain. When the data changes, you need to remember to change it in more than one place. With the relationship, you only change it in the Publication table.

The other reason is that this relationship is much more functional than just saving time and space. It's a two-way relationship you can leverage to display and calculate other fields as we will see next.

Notion automatically created the first of these fields. When you create the relationship from Articles back to Publications, Notion creates a field in the Publications table showing what articles have used that publication. So, doing nothing else, in the Publication table, I have a list of what articles are in each publication, like so.

| Aa Name | | ↗ Related to Medium Artic... | # |
|---|---|---|---|
| a Few Words | | | |
| Ascent | ↗ OPEN | 📄 Photography Taught Me How to Conquer Writer's Block | |
| | | 📄 Someone Else is Buying the Sears Tower Again | |
| | | 📄 Are Grandparents Actual People? | |
| | | 📄 How to Find Things to Look Forward to While Socially Isolated | |
| | | — | |

Next, by using a Rollup property type, I can have the table count the number of articles in each publication for me. To do this, I added another field in the Publications table and called it Count. In the Property Type, I selected Rollup. This is a particular type of field used to count, add, or otherwise "roll-up" another field.

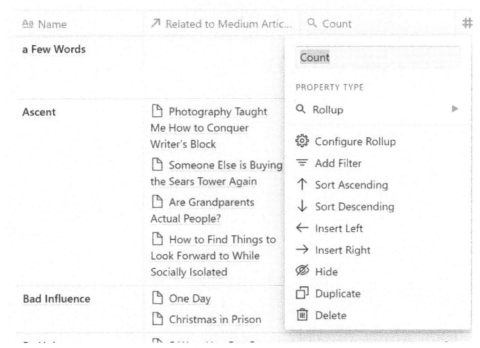

Then, when I clicked on a blank field, I told it to point to the Related to Articles field, use the Property of Title, which is the contents of that field, and then selected Count values as the calculation.

RELATION

↗ Related to Medium Articles (...   ⌄

PROPERTY

Aa Title   ⌄

CALCULATE

Count values   ⌄

Again, you may wonder, why go to that trouble. After all, counting to four isn't that difficult.

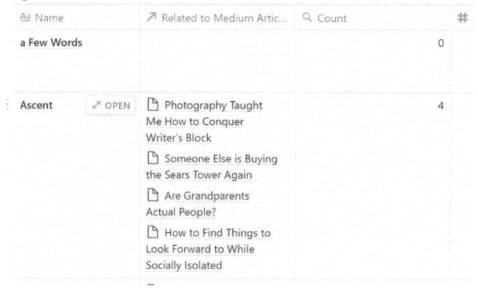

| Aa Name | | ↗ Related to Medium Artic... | Q Count | # |
|---------|---|------------------------------|---------|---|
| a Few Words | | | | 0 |
| Ascent | ↗ OPEN | 📄 Photography Taught Me How to Conquer Writer's Block  📄 Someone Else is Buying the Sears Tower Again  📄 Are Grandparents Actual People?  📄 How to Find Things to Look Forward to While Socially Isolated | | 4 |

Easy for you to say.

But actually, there is another reason to calculate that column. I can then use that calculation in another calculation, and so on. Using the same methods used in the Relation field and the Rollup fields above, I created a field in Publications to grab the Total Revenue field back in Articles. This is a number I enter manually at the end of each month. Then I made a field called Average Per Article, which is of type Function. Using the Total Revenue Relationship field and the Count Rollup field, I created a simple division function that gives me a running total of how much I have made per article for each publication. The number of relationships and the complexity of the calculations are only limited by your imagination. There are many good articles explaining these functions.

I know this sounds complicated, but if you walk through the steps above, it will become very easy. Tables, and especially related tables, give Notion a lot of power you can harness once you get the hang of it.

Whether you use relationships, the other factor that gives tables so much power and flexibility in Notion is the use of Views... and we cover that in another chapter.

I hope this helps, and as always, let me know if you have any questions.

# BONUS MATERIAL:

Notion Mini-Course Bonus Material

Congratulations on buying my mini-course on Notion and for coming this far. I hope you have learned a lot. Notion is both simple and complex, so diving in and playing around is the best way to learn along with my mini-course, of course.

I promised bonus material to everyone who bought the course rather than finding and reading all the separate articles on Medium. You also get a vote in what to include in the next chapter which will be shipped to you for free. Please let me know what else you need to know.

As I said above, Notion has a very active development team. Unlike say, Evernote, updates come very often and usually with much needed or asked for features. So, I thought I would go back to when I first released Chapter One and give a synopsis of interesting features released since then. If you want a full, blow-by-blow of every release, you can find that here.

**Updated and Improved Notifications:** This was in the first update following the pandemic when everyone was scurrying from home. They did a lot of team-centric things in this update, which I am not focusing on, but improved notifications was one of the largest.

**Improved iPad and Android Apps:** I can attest to this. My Android app is much faster, loading in about 10 seconds instead of the 30-40+ before. I can now use the Android app to do speedy things like a quick note to myself or a shopping list without getting impatient.

**Many new templates:** Too numerous to cover, and your use of templates will depend on your particular use cases, but the number available has grown by a ton, just since I started writing this series.

**FREE!!!:** This was the big one, back in May. The personal plan became free. No more 1,000 block limit. IMO, the personal plan now becomes good enough for most people for free. I still ugraded to the Pro plan for two reasons. I don't want to be limited to 5Mb attachments, and more importantly, I want to help this company keep moving forward.

**Nested database filters:** Anyone who has ever written code in SQL will love this. Now you can create more complex database filters such as  Notes where (Type = Standup OR Weekly Sync) AND were created within a week. We database geeks love our and/or logic.

**Inline Math Equations:** You are no longer restricted to using formulas in databases. Turn any properly formatted text into a formula.

**More Team functionality on Mobile:** You no longer have to be on the desktop app to manage and invite team members. Manager your entire team from your phone or tablet.

**Apple Single Sign-In:** Now, sign in with your Apple ID wherever you use Notion, desktop, web, iOS or Android.

**Korean:** Notion, including templates now available in Korean.

**Better Multiple Account Access:** If you manage multiple accounts, you can now switch back and forth without logging out and back in. This was a big time saver while writing the last two chapters of this article. I could jump between my 'real' account and my test account much easier.

**Inline Sub-Pages:** This was another big one for me. I have tons of nested pages. Now they don't have to be on their own line. You can nest a sub-page within a sentence, like any other hyperlink.

**Backlinks:** The folks at Notion definitely pay attention to the competition. Roam Research is the big buzzword this year with backlinks. Now Notion supports the concept. You can now see everywhere the current page is referenced, automatically.

**New Integrations:**
- Abstract
- Miro

---

Notion is one of the most amazing apps to come along in a great while and competitors are scrambling to catch up. It can be confusing at first, but if you've come this far in this mini-course, you should be well on your way.

Make sure you let me know what you want to see in Chapter five by email dbvirago@gmail.com

Thank you for reading.

www.ingramcontent.com/pod-product-compliance
Lightning Source LLC
LaVergne TN
LVHW041220050326
832903LV00021B/722